Woman Mystic

Woman Mystic

Selections from
Saint Hildegard of Bingen's
Scivias

Elizabeth Ruth Obbard

NEW CITY PRESS
OF THE FOCOLARE
Hyde Park, NY

For the Aylesford Choir
Who through their singing
Also join in the praise of God
And the song of life.
And for David our pianist
Thank you

Published in the United States by New City Press
202 Comforter Blvd., Hyde Park, NY 12538
www.newcitypress.com
©2012 Elizabeth Ruth Obbard

Cover design by Leandro De Leon

Library of Congress Cataloging-in-Publication Data

Hildegard, Saint, 1098-1179.
  [Scivias. English. Selections]
  Woman mystic : selections from Hildegard of Bingen's Scivias / [edited by]
Elizabeth Ruth Obbard.
     p. cm.
  ISBN 978-1-56548-463-4 (alk. paper)
  1. Mysticism--Early works to 1800. I. Obbard, Elizabeth Ruth, 1945- II.
Title.
  BV5080.H5413 2012
  248.2'2--dc23

                          2012027824

Printed in the United States of America

Contents

O Fire of the Spirit,
Comforter and advocate,
Life of the life of all creation,
You are holy in giving each form life.

Therefore all praise is yours,
For you are the voice of praise and the joy of
life,
Our hope in highest honor
Offering the prize of light!

Hildegard of Bingen

INTRODUCTION

Hildegard of Bingen (1098–1179), the newly declared Doctor of the Church, is a woman of such formidable accomplishments that one wonders if there was anything she did not master! Hildegard composed music and poetry, produced plays for her community, wrote works on natural science, medicine, theology and hagiography. She also travelled around on preaching tours upbraiding clergy and laity alike, governed her sisters in their day-to-day lives, and kept up an extensive correspondence with the most prominent ecclesiastical and political figures of her time. And she did this within the context of her regular life of prayer, study and work within the Benedictine monastery she founded. She has been called the first woman theologian in the Church and truly merits the title.

Hildegard demonstrates how the monastic life offered women great opportunities for education and the development of natural talents. She is always, and primarily, a Benedictine nun, faithful to the life she has chosen and to her sense of vocation to share what she has received from God. She has a visionary breadth of interest and involvement in both the Divine and natural worlds — a true polymath. Nothing seems to escape either her inner or outer gaze, where everything is directed to the honor and glory of God, as she understands Him.

Hildegard is a woman of grace, of vision, of service, a prophet and teacher par excellence. A woman worth getting to know so as to share something of her insights, even though these belong to a time and place very different from our own.

Life

Hildegard was born in 1098, just as the era of the crusades was beginning. Society at this point was still rather static, everyone "knew their place" in it, and Hildegard's was firmly with the nobility. Her parents, Hildebert and Mechtild, were connected to many noble families, and at the age of eight, their tenth child, Hildegard, was placed with a relative, Jutta, daughter of the Count of Spondheim, who lived as an anchoress. The gift of a child to God was relatively common, especially in large families, and with Jutta, Hildegard lived as a young companion and pupil. From Jutta she learned to read the Bible in Latin and chant the psalms. The hermitage was attached to the abbey of Disibodenberg, and the monks acted as chaplains and spiritual guides. One of them, Volmar, was to become Hildegard's lifelong friend and faithful advocate.

Within a short time other girls and young women gathered around Jutta and Hildegard, and the hermitage was enlarged to become a monastery professing the Rule of St. Benedict. At around the age of fifteen Hildegard made her formal vows, and on the death of Jutta, who had become leader of the community, Hildegard succeeded her. By then she was thirty-eight years old. Five years later she received the prophetic calling which led her to write the *Scivias* and begin her public mission.

Hildegard had experienced both visions and ill health (especially severe migraines) from early childhood, which leads to the strong possibility that her visions and experiences had a physical basis in her own particular temperament and personality. However, this did not stop her living a very active life from middle-age on, and living to what, in her time, would be considered extreme old age (81).

As leader of her nuns Hildegard seems to have grown in confidence and the desire to share some of her insights. With Volmar's encouragement, and after the death of Jutta, she began to write. She also discovered her many other gifts, especially for music, which she soon put to good use, composing over seventy songs and hymns to enrich the liturgical life of her sisters. The independence that came with leadership allowed her creativity to flourish.

Although Hildegard may have lacked a formal education, she seems to have been extremely well read. This enabled her to make connections with many areas of knowledge in an original way, as she was not restricted by categories and theories from other sources. She was insatiably curious, the mark of a mind to which no area of life was closed on principle.

Soon, news of Hildegard's remarkable visionary gifts reached the ears of important ecclesiastics, especially St. Bernard, who confirmed her in her vocation, and the Cistercian Pope, Eugenius III, who authorized her to publish all she had learned from the Holy Spirit. Thus she received official approval for her first and major work *Scivias* or "Know the Ways."

In time Hildegard decided she would like her own independent foundation which, she felt, would remove her from the relative confinements of her present situation in Disibodenberg and give greater scope for her mission. Against the monks' wishes she decided to remove herself to a new monastery situated on the Rupertsberg, some miles away. Building began on the chosen site, and in 1150 Hildegard and twenty of her nuns moved to their new home.

The early years at Rupertsberg were difficult financially, and Hildegard had to insist on a division of assets between Disibodenberg and her new community. At this time she wrote her two works on natural science: *Natural History* and a book called *Causes and Cures*, a medical compendium with a special focus on the needs of women. Another book entitled the *Book of Life's Merits* may reflect her concern over the way life was being lived by the nuns in her convent, as both vices and virtues are depicted in clear and poetic imagery.

Let the sisters take all this to heart! May virtues flourish and vices be eliminated (one can always try for a perfect world!). At the age of sixty, Hildegard embarked on her first preaching tour. And for the next twelve years, precluding periods of serious illness, she made long journeys along the Rhine, speaking to both clergy and lay people with a confidence and clarity that belied her supposed inferiority as a woman. In fact Hildegard never capitalized on her femininity. There is about her an almost masculine assuredness — was she not the mouthpiece of God!

In 1163 Hildegard began her third visionary work, the *Book of Divine Works*. Shortly afterwards she established another foundation of nuns at Eibingen near Rudesheim.

Towards the end of her long life Hildegard showed her true adherence to principle when she allowed a nobleman, who had been excommunicated, to be buried in the monastic cemetery. He had been reconciled with the Church before he died and so, in Hildegard's eyes, was owed a Christian burial. Not so with some church authorities. Rather than look into the situation more closely, they imposed an interdict on the community. Hildegard and her nuns were denied the Sacraments and it was only later, when she had appealed to the Archbishop of Mainz, that the situation was rectified.

Hildegard died peacefully five months later. She was never officially canonized, but in 1342 Pope John XXII gave permission for her cult to be celebrated. Her official status today is of a canonized saint — and now a Doctor of the Church. After many years of relative obscurity Hildegard is once more coming to the fore — like a prophet whose time has arrived.

Hildegard among the women Doctors of the Church

Hildegard joins a relatively small group of women who have been designated Doctors of the Church. This means that their writings are not only considered orthodox, but worthy of being used as guides to the spiritual life by all Christians, both men and women.

The other women Doctors (or teachers) are Catherine of Siena (1347–80), a Dominican Tertiary; Teresa of Avila (1515–82) and Therese of Lisieux (1873–97), the latter both Carmelite nuns. Hildegard predates these other writers, and her approach is quite different. Catherine and Teresa come from the mendicant tradition which has a strong focus on the humanity of Christ and a simple, poor lifestyle. Hildegard is a Benedictine through and through, a woman whose Order's motto is "Peace" and which stresses hierarchy, stability and an ordered day, punctuated by the praise of God in the sung Divine Office. Hence her insistence on such virtues as self-denial, humility and obedience, rather than on the higher reaches of mystical grace.

Catherine is a woman in some respects similar to Hildegard, in that she was ready to travel, to call clergy and laity to account. But she is also very different in that she is primarily focused on a devotional life where Christ and Christ's Blood are paramount in her thinking and in her exhortations. Catherine was devoted to the mystery of Christ's sufferings and passion, and her main work, the *Dialogue* (so called because she presents her teaching in the form of a conversation between herself and God the Father) is wholly Christocentric.

Teresa of Avila, like Hildegard a woman of ill health, visions and many talents, is the great teacher of the stages of prayer. Teresa analyzed the patterns of spiritual growth with the originality and sureness of touch that is the mark of an experienced practitioner. But her works are also shot through with humorous accounts of her foundations, stories of herself and her sisters and the struggle to have her reform recognized by the authorities; not to mention the honest account she gives of her tumultuous and in some respects hectic life. Teresa is altogether a loveable and imitable woman, someone who enjoyed life and laughter as well as having a more serious side to her character.

Therese of Lisieux is a Doctor by virtue of her simple and direct approach to the Gospels, and her witness of a life lived solely for God. She rediscovered the simplicity of the spiritual path as being a life lived with and for Jesus, each moment counting, each small action directed towards God. Therese shows us that every life, no matter how ordinary, has within it the potential for greatness. She is a woman whose focus is love and mercy. She may not have been educated in the normal way (any schooling was over by the time she was fourteen, and at fifteen she was already in Carmel) but her wisdom is immense. Only now are her courage and originality really being fully appreciated.

Hildegard is not a woman one easily loves so much as admires. Her writings are not about the life of prayer or devotion, nor about the spiritual stages along which one walks to union with God. Her visions are not to do with a loving relationship with Christ or Mary. Rather they are truly in the prophetic mold. We will discover more similarities between Hildegard's visions and those of the prophetic Books of Ezekiel or Daniel than we will with our other women mystics. Hildegard's writing is almost completely lacking in gentle or devotional emotion. She is not concerned with love so much as with the whole panorama of the story of salvation. Reason is paramount. Order is necessary. Let no one want to rise above their station in life which has been given by God.

Teresa wanted to offer religious life to any woman who was sincere, no matter what was her family background; whereas for Hildegard noble nuns were those she preferred, as God was only "worthy of the very best." As with any prophet, Hildegard is influenced by the images and symbols around her; all that building work involved in the expansion of Disibodenberg and Rupertsberg, for example, is linked to her visions of buildings. She wants people to relish not just parts of the Biblical story, but to see it whole and interconnected. Hence her great respect for and knowledge of the Old Testament as well as the New.

Hildegard also loves the images of light — a living, bright, shining light, and the adjective "greening," which stands for life and new growth in the Spirit. She is a woman who "sees" and in her seeing seeks a deeper insight into the meaning behind it all.

Scivias

The work I have chosen to concentrate on in this short book is Hildegard's *Scivias*, which means literally "Know the Ways." It is the first of Hildegard's books and is divided into three main sections concerned with the history of salvation.

The theme of Book One is the Creator and Creation.

The theme of Book Two is the Redeemer and Redemption.

The theme of Book Three is the History of Salvation symbolized by a Building.

Within these three Books there are a number of visions related to the main theme and described by Hildegard in great detail. As these visions sound bizarre in many cases it is all the more to her credit that the teaching she draws from them is so reasoned and unemotional.

In Book One the focus is on the time before the coming of Christ, the time of the Old Law (a theme to which she constantly returns in the other Books also).

Book Two presents the theme of the Savior and His presence among us, primarily in the Sacraments of Baptism, Confirmation and Eucharist.

Book Three explores the work of the Spirit in building the kingdom of God here on earth. And it looks at the virtues and their place in our lives if we are to grow in Christ. The work ends with the Day of Judgment and the Song of the Blessed who attain Heaven, a poetic rendering that has been termed the first morality play.

While there are illustrations of the visions in one early manuscript, there is a general consensus that Hildegard is not the artist (at last something it seems she could not do!) so I have felt able to treat these with a certain freedom.

The passages chosen from *Scivias* are personal choices and their rendering is my own, based on the translation by Mother Columba Hart and Jane Bishop.

May Hildegard open the eyes of our minds that we too may benefit from her visions and her sayings.

HILDEGARD DECLARES THE
TRUTH OF HER VISIONS

hen I was forty-three years old, as I was gazing with great attention at a vision of great splendor, I heard a voice saying to me: "Fragile human, poor and timid, speak and write the things you see and hear, not in a human manner that is limited, but according to the will of Him who knows, sees and does all things according to His secret mysteries." And again the heavenly voice told me to speak of the wonders being revealed, and to write them for others. It was the eleven hundred and forty-first year of the Incarnation of the Son of God. I was forty-two years and seven months old when heaven opened and a fiery light of great brilliance filled my brain. It inflamed my heart with the kind of warmth the sun gives when its rays touch something. And immediately I understood the meaning of the Scriptures, both Old and New Testaments, not in detail, but in an amazingly comprehensive manner.

These visions had been with me since I was five years old. They were not dreams nor caused by delirium; rather they came to me while I was fully awake with eyes and ears attuned to the inner self, and with a pure mind. On reaching the age of full maturity it became apparent that now was the time to reveal my visions. God spoke as the Living Light, not enabling me to glory in anything of myself, but to work with the monk Volmar to make hidden things clear. After putting off this command and refusing to write I became sick. Then at last, compelled by the monk Volmar and my dear friend, the nun Richardis of Strade, I began to write.

This book has been in the making for the past ten years. These are indeed the words of God and are about His secret mysteries, which I received in the courts of heaven.

CREATION AND THE FALL

"Then I saw, as it were, a great multitude of very bright
living lamps, which received fiery brilliance and ac-
quired an unclouded splendor ..."

(Hildegard's vision)

The difference between the good and the bad angels

Those who burn with real love for God do not withdraw from Him by any unjust impulse. While those who serve God from pretense, not only fail to advance to greater things but, by God's just judgments, are cast out even from those things which they erroneously presume to possess. This is shown by the great multitude of very bright, living lamps, which are the vast army of heavenly spirits, shining in the blessed life, and living in great beauty and adornment.

When they were created, they did not place themselves in any prideful position, but persisted strongly in divine love. They received an unclouded splendor because, while Lucifer and his followers attempted to rebel against God and embraced the torpor of ignorance, they clothed themselves in the vigilance of divine love. At the fall of the Devil great praise burst forth from these angelic spirits. They realized clearly that God is unchangeable and unconquerable. And so, burning with love and persevering in doing right, they despised all the dust of injustice.

The human condition symbolized by a garden, a sheep, and a pearl

A good master planning a garden chooses a suitable site and, before planting, decides which is the best area for the plants he wishes to flourish there. And being wise he encloses the garden within a heavy wall so that enemies cannot cause havoc. He then appoints experts who know how to water a garden and collect its fruit, making from that fruit many sweet-smelling things. Surely if the master foresaw that the garden would bring forth no fruit, but would ultimately be destroyed, why would he have planted, watered and fortified it with so much labor and care?

Listen then to this interpretation:

God is the Sun of Justice who made His splendor rise over human wickedness and filth. That Sun shone so brightly that the filth stank and became putrefied. Because of this those looking at the sun loved it even more because of its contrast with the filth.

Human wickedness is like that filth compared with the beauty of the sun of God's justice.

A sheep, belonging to the master who had planted the garden, fell into the filth. This was by its own choice, not the master's neglect. The master however sought it again with justice and energy.

The meaning of this is that the innocent Lamb was suspended on the cross, slain by murderers. This enabled the lost sheep to be brought back to the pastures of life. The devil did not know this Lamb but only recognized him after redemption had been completed.

The devil, the persecutor, when first created, raised himself up in pride and expelled Man from Paradise and its glory. But God did not want to resist the devil by exerting His power. Instead He chose to do so by the humility of His Son. In this way the lost sheep was brought back to life.

Why then are you so hard-hearted you humans? God did not forsake you but sent his Son for your salvation, thus crushing the pride of the serpent. Hell's gate was opened and humanity snatched from death, making the devil's cohorts marvel at such a power.

Thus humanity was lifted above the heavens because God appeared in Man, and Man in God.

It was as if the master brought the precious sheep back to life. Or as if a precious pearl had slipped from his grasp and fallen into the mud. But the master drew the pearl up from the dirt and purified it of the filth in which it had lain, giving it even greater glory and honor.

For God created humanity, but humanity fell into death through the devil's instigation. The Son of God then saved humanity by his blood and brought it gloriously to heaven.

How did he do this? By humility and by love.

Why humility and love are greater than all other virtues

Humility caused the Son of God to be born of the humble Virgin, a maiden not eager for fleshly embraces, gold ornaments or earthly honors. Thus the Son of God lay in a poor manger, born of a poor woman.

The work of humility is to groan, weep and take no notice of offences.

Therefore, whoever wants to conquer the devil must be armed with humility. Satan flees from humility and hides from it like a snake in a hole.

Wherever humility finds the devil it snaps him, breaking him as if he were a fragile thread.

Love took the Only-Begotten Son from the bosom of the Father in heaven and placed Him in the womb of an earthly mother; for love does not spurn sinners or publicans but wants to save everyone.

Love can make tears flow and soften hard hearts.

Humility and love are brighter than other virtues in that they are like a soul and body with stronger powers than other bodily members.

Humility is like the soul.

Love is like the body.

These work together in an inseparable way just as soul and body are inseparable as long as we are alive.

The parts of the body are subject according to their powers to the whole body and soul, so all other virtues cooperate with humility and love.

Therefore, humans, for God's glory and your personal salvation, pursue humility and love. If you are armed with them you have no need to fear the snares of the devil. Instead you already are assured of everlasting life.

(Book 1: Vision 2)

VISION OF THE TRINITY

"Then I saw a bright light, and in the light the figure of a man the color of sapphire which was all blazing with a gentle glowing fire ..."

(Hildegard's vision)

On the Three Persons in One God

Then I heard the living Light saying to me:
You see a bright light which in all its perfection stands for the Father.

And in this light is a figure the color of sapphire which is without flaw. This stands for the Son. He was begotten by the Father from all eternity, and within time became incarnate in the world through his humanity, which is all blazing with a gentle glowing fire.

This fire, without any darkness or imperfection, stands for the Holy Spirit, by whom the Only-Begotten Son was conceived of the Virgin within time, and poured his true light into the world.

The bright light, the glowing fire, bathe each other in brightness and flow over the human figure, so that the three are one light in one power of potential.

This means that the Father, who is justice, is not without Son or Holy Spirit.

The Holy Spirit who enkindles our hearts is not without the Father or the Son.

The Son, who is the plenitude of all things, is not without the Father or the Holy Spirit.

They are inseparable in Divine Majesty.

Let no one ever forget to pray to Me, the only God in these Three Persons, because it was for this that I made them known to you — that you may burn more ardently in My love; since it was for love of humanity that I sent My Son into the world.

God has not forgotten or turned from the human race.

God has in mercy remembered His great work and His precious pearl, Man, formed from the mud of the earth, and into whom God breathed the breath of life.

And how has He done this?

He has devised for us the life of penitence which is unfailingly efficacious. Humanity was deceived by the serpent. But God cast humanity into penitence, which calls for humility, and this the devil cannot practice.

Salvation did not spring from our own merits, we were ignorant and incapable of loving God. But the Creator and Lord of all so loved His people that He sent His Son for their salvation. He it is who has washed and dried our wounds.

From Him flows the sweetest balm containing all good things.

Stone, flame and word

Father, Son and Holy Spirit are indivisible in the Unity of the Divinity, as can be seen from the qualities of a stone, a flame and a word.

The qualities of a stone are:

1) Cool dampness, meaning that it cannot be dissolved or broken.
2) Solidity to the touch, that it may be used to build houses and defenses.
3) Sparkling fire, that it may be heated and become consolidated in hardness.

The cool dampness signifies the Father, Who never withers and whose power never ends. Solidity of touch stands for the Son, Who was born of the Virgin and could be touched and known.

The sparkling fire stands for the Holy Spirit who enkindles and enlightens the hearts of the faithful.

This signifies that if a bodily person continually touches the dampness of stone, such a one will become sick and weak. In the same way one who rashly tries to contemplate the Father in unsteady thoughts loses faith.

As people build their dwellings to defend themselves against enemies, through the solidity of stone buildings, so the Son of God, the true Cornerstone, is the dwelling of faithful people and a protector from evil spirits.

As sparkling fire lights up dark places by burning what it touches, so the Holy Spirit drives out unbelief and consumes sin.

And as these three qualities are in one stone, so the true Trinity is in one Unity.

The qualities of a flame

As the flame of a fire has three qualities so there is one God in three Persons.

A flame is made up of:

1) brilliant light, that it may shine,
2) red power, that it may endure,
3) fiery heat, that it may burn.

By the brilliant light I understand the Father, Who in fatherly love opens His brightness to His faithful.

By the red power which makes the flame strong I understand the Son, Who took on a human body from the Virgin in which divine wonders were shown.

By the fiery heat I understand the Holy Spirit, Who burns in the minds of the faithful.

A flame is only seen where there is brilliant light, red power and fiery heat.

Only where Father, Son and Holy Spirit are known, only there can God be properly worshipped.

The three causes of human words

In a word there is sound, meaning and breath.
Sound that it may be heard.
Meaning that it may be understood.
Breath that it may be spoken.

The sound is the Father, who shows all things with ineffable power.

The meaning is the Son, miraculously begotten of the Father.

The breath is the Holy Spirit who sweetly burns in them.

Where no sound is heard, no meaning used, no breath breathed, no word will be understood. So also Father, Son and Spirit are undivided and always work together.

(Book 2: Vision 2)

THE CHURCH, BRIDE OF CHRIST AND MOTHER OF THE FAITHFUL

"After this I saw the image of a woman as large as a great city, with a wonderful crown on her head and arms from which hung a splendor like sleeves. Her womb was pierced like a net with many openings, with a huge multitude of people running in and out. And that image spreads out its splendor like a garment, saying, "I must conceive and give birth."

(Hildegard's vision)

The Woman, image of the Church

You see the image of the woman as large as a great city; this designates the Bride of my Son who always bears her children by regeneration in the Spirit and in water.

She has a wonderful crown on her head for at her beginning, when she was raised up by the blood of the Lamb, she was fittingly adorned with apostles and martyrs. Thus she was betrothed with true betrothal to My Son, since in His blood she faithfully formed herself into a firm building of holy souls.

Her womb is pierced like a net, displaying her maternal kindness at capturing faithful souls by various goads of virtue in this net, trusting people live their lives by faith. The One who casts the net to capture the fishes is My Son, the Bridegroom of His beloved

Church, whom He betrothed to Himself in His blood to repair the fall of lost humanity.

The Sacraments: Baptism and Confirmation

Baptism

The Jewish people received circumcision in one bodily member, but I want all men and women to be circumcised in all their members.

A new circumcision, that of baptism sprang from the Baptism of My Son. It will remain until the last day, abiding for eternity and knoowing no end.

Those circumcised in the washing of baptism will be truly saved if they also do good deeds. For I will receive anyone, young or old, who has kept my covenant, believing in Me and confessing the Trinity, either personally or through a godparent if they should be infants or otherwise unable to speak for themselves.

Words of the Gospel

"Whoever believes and is baptized shall be saved; whoever does not believe will be condemned" (Mark 16:16). This means that a person who sees by an inner eye what is hidden from outer sight is one who has faith. For what is seen outwardly is known outwardly. What is seen inwardly is understood inwardly.

> *God is unseen to human eye,*
> *but perceived in the mirror of faith.*

The spirit of such a person seeks true loftiness and feels the new life offered by the Son of Man, who was conceived by the Holy Spirit, through His mother who received him from the mystery of the Father.

As humanity was born in the flesh, as Adam when created by the divine power, so the Holy Spirit revives the life of the soul by a pouring out of water.

The Divinity receives into itself a person's spirit, restoring life as one is first brought to life in a wave of blood from another human body.

And just as the human form is then lovingly formed and called human, so now the soul is brought to new life in water before the eyes of God, so that God knows His own as an inheritor of life.

I have not excluded any race from my salvation, but through my Son I have mercifully made my calling available to everyone. For whatever age or sex persons may be when coming to baptism, I will receive them with my merciful help.

Infants I receive as well, just as in the Old Testament I accepted infant circumcision, even though the child did not ask by itself; rather faith was supplied by the parents. It is the same in infant baptism.

The Ceremony of Baptism

In honor of the Trinity there should be three people at the font: the priest, who officiates and pours the water; and the two godparents, who speak the words of faith. Because of the spiritual relationship formed by being a godparent, a godparent cannot marry anyone for whom they have spoken the words of faith at baptism.

In the Baptism of my Son, I the Father thundered, which is enacted when the priest speaks the words and gives the blessing for the washing.

The Holy Spirit, seen in the form of a gentle dove, is symbolized by the man who speaks to and teaches the one being baptized in simplicity of heart.

My Son was baptized in the flesh. And the flesh is symbolized in the woman who stands by in the sweetness of a nurturer.

Growing in Baptismal faith

As a baby is nourished bodily by milk, and the food prepared for it by another, so a person must observe the faith given in baptism.

For if a baby does not take its mother's breast or eat the food ground up for it, it will die.

So also if a baptized person does not receive the nurturing love of mother Church, or retain the words of faithful teachers, the soul will die, having refused salvation and the sweetness of eternal life.

A master gives orders to a servant in a commanding voice, and the servant obeys in fear and trembling.

Likewise a mother teaches her daughter to love, and the daughter fulfills her words in obedience in the same way. So let those who have vowed the faith offer words of salvation at the right time, that they may be carried out with devotion for the love of heaven.

Anyone can baptize in necessity

If someone is dying and no priest can be found, anyone who pours the water while invoking the Trinity truly baptizes and the person baptized will receive remission of all their sins and the grace of heavenly blessedness.

But the Trinity must be invoked or the baptism is invalid.

Therefore let all who want to be saved not neglect this sacrament. For they can only receive life from their mother the Church, as does an infant from its human mother.

(Book 2: Vision 3)

Confirmation

After the light of baptism, which arose with Jesus the Sun of Justice, the new Bride of the Lamb, the Church, was adorned and made whole by the gift of the Holy Spirit.

So also each baptized person should be confirmed by a bishop's anointing, so that they will be strengthened and fully adorned for blessedness and justice.

Only a bishop can confirm because only he can confer the Spirit, and the Church is perfected by the gifts of the Holy Spirit, whose fire brings forth and kindles true doctrine in Christians.

Those who stand by as sponsors to confirmation candidates are joined in the Spirit and cannot then enter marriage together. For the sponsor who holds the candidate's hand symbolizes faith, which does not seek the things of the flesh but always the things pertaining to the Spirit.

Three ways in which the Church resounds like a trumpet.

The Church cries out:
"Fear the Father,

Love the Son.
Burn in the Holy Spirit."

This cry is given to her by me, the Father, in the Son, through the Holy Spirit.

So I, God the Father, am reminded by the Son to spare human sin, which by penitence can be forgiven, because the Son took on humanity while himself being sinless, conceived and born without any fleshly stain.

So He receives sinners purified by sorrow for sin because He is God. And then the Church too turns back to her children and cherishes them with a mother's love.

(Book 2: Vision 4)

THE MYSTICAL BODY OF THE CHURCH

"After this I saw that a splendor white as snow and translucent as crystal had shone around the woman from the top of her head to her throat. And from her throat to her navel another splendor, red in color, had encircled her, glowing like the dawn from her throat to her breasts and shining from her breasts to her navel mixed with purple and blue ..."

(Hildegard's vision)

Apostles and priests

The splendor, white as snow and translucent as crystal, that shines around the image of the woman (who symbolizes the Church) stands for the incorrupt Bride surrounded by apostolic teaching.

The apostolic teaching shone first when the apostles began to preach, building up the Church and incorporating workers who would strengthen the Catholic faith: priests, bishops, and all in clerical orders.

The priests are like those of the Old Law, who were appointed to feed the multitudes with spiritual food.

The apostles also chose those same orders under heavenly inspiration.

These travelled to other lands, carrying the anointing chrism and announcing the law to the people.

They are stewards carefully chosen to teach the people and distribute the food of life.

Their lives therefore should reflect their teaching as shepherds of My sheep, and they should offer the spotless sacrifice prefigured in the offering of the innocent Abel.

Example of Abel

Abel offered the firstlings of his flock and his innocent life pleased God. And as he was in charge of pasturing and guarding the flock with simple devotion, so let the chrism-makers (bishops) who are set over the children of the Church (who are the sheep of Christ) pasture them according to His plan, faithfully feed them with His words, and teach them to live by Church rules, protecting them from the snares of the evil one.

The fruit they then offer to God will be like the first fruits offered by Abel.

Ministers of the Church should therefore live blameless and chaste lives; for how can one who lives a corrupt life heal others?

The place of virgins and monks in the Church

Neither the order of virgins, nor that of monks, nor others that imitate them such a desert hermits, are commanded under the Old Law.

In due time the apostles announced the gospel way of salvation, and the bright dawn of the daughters of Sion arose in the love of my Son; that is, the dawn of those who repressed the flesh with vigor and harshly mortified their evil desires.

As chaste virginity followed my Son with ardent love, the order of monks imitated His Incarnation.

These are my true temples, where it is as if I am worshipped by choirs of angels. They bear in their bodies the Passion, death and burial of the Only-Begotten in renouncing the will of the flesh and separating themselves from all worldly adornment.

Example of John the Baptist

"The same John had a garment of camel's hair and a leather girdle about his loins" (Matt 3:4).

This means that Divine grace had awakened him to a miraculous abstinence, and that by grace his virtue was made sure.

For in his mind John had despised all earthly honors and riches, and he had mortified his body by restraints against fleshly pleasure.

A life consisting of hard and rough ways enabled him to build greater towers of virtue than any of those who went before him.

And he did this especially by an ardent love of chastity, and by showing the way of healing to those who sought it.

Therefore all professed monks should follow John's way of life, fleeing from worldly things, restraining the mind, and renouncing evil desires.

This makes it possible for them to shine more brightly than those who have gone before them by simply walking in God's ways. Rather, these spiritual athletes (monks and virgins) take the steep and narrow path by firmly treading underfoot the pleasures of the world.

Like the angels they neither seek nor long for earthly things.

Monks encircle the Church like a strong girdle. They are concerned with My Son's Incarnation and, like the angels, sing joyful melodies or pray in sorrow.

These are my strong, loving people, for in them I contemplate my Son in His suffering; and they die His death when they obey their superiors for the sake of eternal life.

How lay people too adorn the Church

Secular life surrounds the Church with a pure and calm purpose, with all reverence, helping to build up the Body of Christ in strength and virtue.

The whole human race has come from the womb of the Church. Here she gathers rich and poor, rulers and subjects and all humanity of whatever class or sex.

Lay people who keep the law of God are a wonderful adornment when they obey superiors with sincere humility and devotion, give alms, chastise their bodies for God's love, and embrace continence, widowhood and other good works. By these things they embrace God and are most loveable to Me.

The bond of marriage

"Whoever God has joined together let no one separate" (Matt 19:6).

This means that God, in creating the human race, took flesh from flesh (Eve from Adam) and joined them in union.

This connection must not be broken easily or in foolish haste, for flesh to flesh, blood to blood, are made one in a legal ceremony.

Both may dissolve this bond for a just cause or because of devotion to God, but it must not be done lightly.

For God instituted this bond for the propagation of the human race, therefore one should not mingle one's blood with that of another outside marriage.

Guard the love for your spouse, that your inner self may not be wounded by carelessness or lust.

Conclusion

These orders surround and consolidate the Church, wondrously honoring the Blessed Trinity, causing her to bud and be fruitful with blessed greening.

Within her many steps and ladders are properly placed for the varieties of lay people and religious.

By means of these the Church guides her children to faithfully fulfill the precepts proper to their state of life, and to yearn for heavenly rather than earthly things.

(Book 2: Vision 5)

CHRIST'S SACRIFICE AND THE CHURCH

"And after these things I saw the Son of God hanging on the cross, and the aforementioned woman coming forth like a bright radiance from the ancient counsel. By divine power she was led to Him, and she raised herself upward so that she was sprinkled by the blood from His side. And thus, by the will of the Heavenly Father, she was joined with Him in happy betrothal and nobly dowered with His body and blood ..."

(Hildegard's vision)

The Church — God's betrothed

When Jesus Christ hung on the cross the Church, joined to Him in the secret mysteries of heaven, took as her wedding dowry His precious blood.

At the altar she reclaims her wedding gift, noting how her children receive that gift when they come to celebrate the sacred mysteries.

Jesus conquered the serpent through humility, not power and strength, and He gave his body and blood to make holy those who believe.

The analogy of gold

As a goldsmith melts pieces of gold in the fire, and then divides the gold when it has become one piece, so I, the Father, first glorify the body and blood of my Son through the Holy Spirit, and then distribute it to the faithful for their healing and salvation.

And when the priest approaches the altar to offer the holy sacrifice of the Lamb, a great light from heaven drives away the darkness, for here is true food for the soul by which believers are saved.

And just as the body of the Son of God, when buried in the tomb, was raised to life from the sleep of death, so the same Son covers over the sacrificial offering so that people see only bread and wine; just as the divinity of the Son was hidden during his earthly life.

Analogy of a chick and a butterfly

For as a chick emerges from an egg, or a butterfly springs from a cocoon, and the living creature flies away while the thing it came from remains, so also in this oblation. The truth that My Son's body and blood are present must be held by faith, though all that appears to human sight is bread and wine.

The Lord's Prayer

Until the world ends I will see in the Passion all who believe or reject this offering. This offering shines before Me as long as people pray the Lord's prayer.

"Forgive us our debts as we forgive our debtors" (Matt 6:12). We have not fulfilled what we promised at our Baptism for we have sinned and lost our innocence. But You are kind. Forgive us our sins according to Your loving kindness.

Hear this then! As long as you need help and as long as you can help others, My Son's Passion shall appear before Me in mercy, and His body and blood will be here to be received by believers for their salvation and the remission of their sins.

Why bread and wine are offered

The grain of wheat is the strongest and best of all fruits. It has in its stalk neither sap nor pith like other trees, but its stem rises in a spike that leads to the fruit.

It never produces bitter fruit, either in heat or cold, but yields dry flour.

So too the flesh of My Son was dry, with nothing polluted as in the rest of the human race. My Only-Begotten came forth in verdant integrity as the stalk brings forth the clustered grain, coming from the Virgin's womb in simple innocence.

From His mother He drew no sap of sin, because she conceived Him without the pith of a man, being overshadowed by the Holy Spirit in purity.

Wine comes from the vine, and the blood of My Son flowed from His side as the grape drips from the vine.

And as the grape is trodden by feet and crushed in the winepress, giving sweet wine to strengthen human blood, so during His agony and Passion life-giving blood issued from My Son's wounds, sprinkling believers with life-giving freedom.

The grape is unlike other fruit in that people usually suck grapes rather than eat them. Their delicate texture is like the flesh of My Son, uncontaminated by sin.

For as wine flows out of the vine, so My Son was the true Vine, and from Him many branches went forth. For the faithful are planted in Him, and through Him bring forth the fruit of good works.

Those who faithfully cleave to Him are made by Him green and fruitful, bringing forth fruits of noble virtue. Just as He too, being sweet and mild, brought forth precious offshoots in holiness and justice, and cleansed believers from every stain. As it says in the Song of Songs: "A cluster of grapes of Cyprus is my beloved to me in the vineyards of Engedi" (Song 1:13).

Why water and wine are mixed together in the sacrament

Water must be added to the wine because blood and water issued from the side of My Son. His Divinity is understood by the wine, His humanity is understood by the water.

My Only-Begotten, the fountain of living water, cleansed people by new life in the Spirit and made them ready for heaven, as it is written, "I, like a river channel and like an aqueduct, came forth from Paradise" (Eccl 24:41).

When humanity was seduced by the deceiver and fell into death, the Only-Begotten Son poured Himself out in the agony of His Passion. He willed to suffer for the human race in His body. During His agony His blood came out in drops of sweat. Then on the cross, water with blood flowed from the wound in His side.

But in this sacrifice the wine must be more abundant than the water, for blood surpasses the liquid that dilutes it, just as milk exceeds the watery substance that moistens it.

Therefore, you faithful who eat this bread, drink also this wine with pure purpose.

(Book 2: Vision 6)

THE HISTORY OF SALVATION SYMBOLIZED BY A BUILDING

" ... 𝔄nd on that mountain stood a four-sided building, formed in the likeness of a four walled city; it was
placed at an angle so that one of its corners faced the
𝔈ast, one faced the 𝔚est, one the 𝔑orth and one the
𝔖outh ..."

(Hildegard's vision)

Faith from Abraham
to the Incarnation

𝔉aith appeared faintly in the saints of the Old Testament. But at the Incarnation of the Son of God
it burst into burning light. For the Son of God did
not want passing things; and He taught by example
that they should be trampled underfoot and heavenly
things loved in their place.

The early patriarchs did not separate themselves
from the world, for it had not yet been shown them
that they should forsake all things. Rather, they worshipped God with simple faith and humble devotion.

Faith first appeared with the circumcision of Abraham, and progressed until the coming of God's Son,
the Supreme One.

Since the ancient serpent was ruined, this faith has
been inspired in people by the Holy Spirit, faithfully

working in the Father, enabling them to believe that God is almighty.

For God has indeed conquered the great enemy and, sustained by this belief, people can attain the glory from which the Devil was barred by his pride.

The four-sided building of salvation

The goodness of the Father builds good works on faith.

Gathering multitudes from the four corners of the earth, He draws them to heavenly things and makes them strong and constant in virtue.

Then the Heavenly Father graciously places them in His bosom (which is His inner power and mystical counsel) in four categories of faith:

First, the race of Adam.

Second, the coming of Noah.

Third, the time of Abraham, Moses and the Law.

And last, the time of the Holy Trinity when the Old Testament was openly fulfilled in the Son of God.

The symbolism of the corners

The corner that faces East stands for the Son of God, born of the Virgin and who suffered in the flesh that justice might arise in humanity.

The Western corner stands for the time from Abel to the coming of the Son. It symbolizes the observance of the physical laws of the Old Testament.

The Northern corner stands for the faithful people arising from Abraham and Moses, who foreshadowed the promised grace through which humanity would be saved and the Devil put to flight.

The Southern corner stands for the human race nobly and beautifully restored by the work of God and man bearing full fruit.

(Book 3: Vision 2)

The divine virtue put forth by the Law bear fruit in the Gospel

By the strength and constancy of God's will, the divine virtues sprang up gradually in the Old Testament. But to those who revered them in near ignorance they did not taste wholly sweet and delightful.

For then the Law was seen only as a correction for the erring. But these virtues brought forth much fruit in the new Law, showing the hungry the sweetest, strongest and most perfect food, which is the love of heavenly things.

The foreshadowing of God's will was revealed in many different ways and meanings in the circumcision.

(Book 3: Vision 3)

THE FIGURES OF HEAVENLY LOVE, DISCIPLINE, MODESTY, MERCY AND VICTORY

"After this I looked, and behold! In the middle of the shining part of the building's outer wall there stood an iron-colored tower which was built out from the outer side. It was four cubits wide and seven cubits high. In it I saw five figures standing separately, each in its own arch with a conical tower above it."

(Hildegard's vision)

The meaning of the five figures

In this tower (that is, the strength of the circumcision) there are five strong virtues. For humanity is perfected by virtues, which are the deeds of people working in God.

These five virtues stand in the tower in the likeness of a person's five senses.

Zealously they seized upon the circumcision, cutting it off from all iniquity, as the five senses are circumcised in the Church by baptism.

But the virtues do not work in a person automatically, but only with the person's consent (as do the senses), that virtues and senses may bear fruit together.

The five figures resemble each other, which is to say that they worship God in human deeds with equal devotion. Each is dressed in silk garments, for each of these virtues is sweet, delightful and unconstraining.

They are shod in white shoes for they follow My justice in righteousness and heavenly purity, trampling out all traces of the devil in human beings.

The figure of Celestial Love

The first figure signifies Celestial Love, for this love must exist in a person before anything else.

On her head she wears a bishop's miter and has long white hair. This shows that Celestial Love was crowned in the High Priest Jesus Christ, but also in the high priests of the Old Testament and in those who called to the Son of God in the words of the prophet, "Oh, that you would rend the heavens and come down" (Is 64:1). She stands without a woman's head covering so that her hair flows freely and its whiteness is visible.

By this hair she prefigures the freeing of the priesthood from the bonds of marriage by the coming of My Son.

For His priests should, for the sake of salvation, imitate Him in His chastity; holding to perfect love and shaking off every evil action.

She wears a white pallium whose two borders are adorned on the inside with embroidered purple. This shows that the grace of God surrounds her in gentle purity.

In her right hand she holds lilies and other flowers. This means that for her good works she is rewarded with the lilies of eternal life, light and holiness.

In her left hand she carries a palm, which has grown out of the secret virtue that remembers death. With it she can stop death as if by rolling stones in its path.

The figure of Discipline

The second figure represents Discipline. For, after the love of heavenly things has been instilled in a person, carnal lust must be restrained by the discipline of sorrow for sin.

She is clothed in a purple tunic, for she is surrounded by my Law and the mortification of the flesh.

The purple garment is the example of My Son, born of the Virgin in love, who gives discipline the means of working.

She stands like a youth who has not yet attained adulthood but is very serious. For Discipline is always full of childlike fear, like a child under restraint who respects the schoolmaster — Myself, the Almighty, the master of discipline.

In Me she does not appear as an adult, in that she does not try to use power to do her own will, but faithfully and reverently fears.

The figure of Modesty

The third figure represents Modesty, for modesty appears after discipline to blush and drive away sin.

So she covers her face with the white sleeve on her right arm. For she protects her inner conscience, the face of her soul, by fleeing fornication and the Devil's pollution.

She defends herself with the white garment of innocence and chastity, on the right hand of which is the salvation arising from her good deeds.

The figure of Mercy

The fourth figure signifies Mercy. For after modesty the virtue of mercy appears to help the needy.

In the heart of the Father is true, gracious mercy, which He ordained from eternity and showed first to Abraham.

For He led him forth from his land and commanded that he and his race should be circumcised.

He showed him great wonders in the true Trinity, and through this He symbolically foreshadowed His Son, and foreshadowed mercy in the sacrifice of Isaac.

This figure has her head veiled in womanly fashion with a white veil. For one who has mercy can bring back lost souls to the pure protection of the holy veil, sheltering them from the evil of exile and death.

Mercy makes souls white and people radiant, as they are covered with God's mercy.

So those who disdained God while they were sinning will find Him shining on them like a gentle sunbeam when Mercy is brought to them from heaven.

So Mercy, in the figure of a woman, is a fruitful mother of souls.

As a woman covers her head, so Mercy averts the death of souls. As women are sweeter than men, so Mercy is sweeter than the great sin in a sinner before being visited by God.

Mercy appears in feminine form because sweetness arose in the womb of the Virgin Mary. For Mercy dwelt first with the Father, but became visible through the Holy Spirit in the womb of the Virgin.

Mercy wears a yellow cloak for she is surrounded by the shining sun symbolizing my Son.

On her breast she has a picture of Him, for I put my Son on the breast of Mercy when I sent Him into the womb of the Virgin Mary. Therefore around the picture is written "Through the depths of the mercy of our God the morning sun has come to visit us" (Luke 1:78).

The figure of Victory

The fifth figure stands for Victory. For after the mercy I showed by the circumcision when I willed to send My Son into the world, the same circumcision gave rise to victory, which went on increasing until the coming of My Son, and continues with Him until the last day.

Among the virtues the first is celestial love, which consists in a person knowing and loving God above all things.

Then the person, because of faith, is bound by the law of discipline.

From there he goes on to repress any tendency to sin through good and righteous modesty.

And with these three powers the person soon becomes a strong soldier, imitating my Son, the true Samaritan, in mercy.

And lastly he wins victory over the power of the Devil with the arms of virtue and true humility.

Victory, the fifth virtue, is armed with a helmet on her head, for we should long for God, the Head of all things.

She is arrayed in a breastplate, so that we might resist the Devil by restraining carnal desire.

This virtue is also wearing greaves, so that when she sees the right path she can leave the way of death by chastising the body. She wears iron gloves to escape the Devil and avoid the snares of the cruel enemy.

A shield hangs from her left shoulder, for the left is the side of the Devil's combat with humanity, so she is surrounded with the grace of God's mighty precepts.

She is girded with a sword to cut away iniquity, and holds a spear in her right hand to overcome the Devil's filth with the peace of the Lord.

Under her feet is a lion, with its mouth open. This is the Devil, laid low by Victory.

Its tongue is hanging out which represents his plan to devour the whole human race descended from Adam.

Some people also stand under her feet. These are like flutes upon which the Devil can play his evil tunes. While Victory, acting justly, strikes them down.

Some of the people beneath her are blowing trumpets for they are drunk with the sound of evil.

Some are fooling with instruments used in shows, for they try to deceive the Devil and stubbornly hold to their twisted pride.

Others are playing different games, caught in their own filth – a filth not of their own choosing (as they suppose) but corrupted by the snares of the Devil.

And Victory tramples the lion and all these people under her feet, for with great zeal and divine justice she crushes all these vanities of human art and diabolical persuasion.

At the same time she pierces them with the spear in her right hand, for with the confidence and daring she derives from God, she pierces, conquers and wounds all these impurities.

(Book 3: Vision 3)

THE ZEAL OF GOD

"After this I looked, and behold! In the north corner, where the building's two kinds of walls joined, there appeared a head of marvelous form, planted firmly by the neck at the outside of the corner... And this head was fiery in color, sparkling like a fiery flame; and it had a terrible human face, which looked in great anger towards the North... And it had three wings of wondrous breadth and length, white like a cloud ..."

(Hildegard's vision)

God's jealousy and what it does

God worked His jealousy very severely on the people of the Old Law; but towards those of the New, for love of His Son, He was mild and sweet.

This is not because He carelessly dismissed or overlooked the sins committed, but because He was mercifully awaiting the true inner penitence of the pure heart.

At the same time He refused to tolerate the sins of the hardened, but punished them with just judgment.

Therefore the head that you see in the north corner symbolizes the Jealousy of the Lord, which punishes the inflexible iniquity that does not want to be cured.

This jealousy was prefigured in the symbols of the patriarchs and prophets, and arose openly in the mystery of the Word of God.

The Way of Life and the Way of Death

All people have within themselves two competing callings:

A desire for fruit.

The lust for vice.

By the desire for fruit one is called towards life, and by the lust for vice one is orientated towards death.

The desire for fruit makes people want to do good, saying to themselves "Do good works." Thus they avoid evil and produce useful fruit.

But in the lust for vice, people want to do evil, saying to themselves, "Do whatever pleases you."

In the latter there is a refusal to resist evil, and a delight in vicious behavior. Thus I, God, am treated as an imposter. It is as David says in the psalms:

"They have set their mouths against Heaven, and their tongue has passed over the earth" (Psalm 72:9).

How people addicted to vice behave

Many people are foolish in their understanding and unwilling to admit to the need of practicing the fear of the Lord. They cast aside the good desires they should have for Me, and any knowledge of the true God.

They disregard the knowledge that helps people perform good works in God. Instead they hug bitterness to themselves and contradict the good.

Instead of laying up good treasures they lay up multiple sins.

In these sins they apply their twisted minds to heavenly works and, speaking evil, destroy what is good in rage and mockery.

They mock the teachings of the Old Testament as irrelevant, whereas I established these people Myself in the way of Heavenly works.

Human choice, reason, and the fiery grace of Christ

It is God who works in you whatever is good, because He has made you in such a way that, when you act with wisdom and discretion, you feel Him in your reason.

A natural animal is without intellect or wisdom, without discretion or shame. A mere creature feels God but does not know Him.

The rational animal, that is the human person, has intellect and wisdom, discretion and shame, and acts in ways that are rooted in reason.

Reason is the first root fixed by God's grace in everyone who is given life and a soul.

Good powers flourish where there is reason, for good powers make people know God and choose what is just.

Therefore the deed that a person embraces in the Savior, the Son of God, through whom the Father works in the Holy Spirit, is productive, perfect and prosperous.

And the fiery grace of Christ Jesus recalls this deed to a person's mind and enkindles new enthusiasm for acting.

The need to perform works of justice

Let each person perform works of justice in the joy of the Holy Spirit, not hesitating or grumbling.

Let no one think themselves lacking in anything when they have within themselves the root of God's gift, and the fiery grace of the Holy Spirit to admonish them should they fall into vice.

One who is turned towards Me is alert to the danger of falling into perverse and compulsive behavior, thus weakening the interior root.

Be careful not to distrust God. Avoid evil, and thus avoid the resulting tearful laments that surely follow.

(Book 3: Vision 5)

THE STONE WALL OF
THE OLD LAW

"And the figure that stood on the wall at the same end was bareheaded, with curly black hair and a swarthy face. She was dressed in a tunic of many different colors. And I saw that she took off the tunic and her shoes, and stood naked. And suddenly her hair and her face gleamed newly white, like a newborn baby, and her whole body shone like light. And then I saw on her breast a splendid cross with the image of Christ Jesus. It was depicted above a little bush with two flowers on it, a lily and a rose, which reached upwards towards the cross. And I saw her vigorously shake the tunic and shoes she had taken off, so that a great deal of dust flew out of them."

(Hildegard's vision)

Words of Salvation

The figure in the vision said to me: "I take off the Old Testament, and I put on the noble Son of God with His holiness and truth. And thus I am restored to my good deeds and stripped of my vices."

As I looked attentively at these things the One seated on the throne said to me:

"No Christian should refuse to submit to government, prefigured in the Old Law."

The necessity of obeying human authority

Let none of the faithful who humbly wish to obey God hesitate to submit to the human institutions of government.

Through the Holy Spirit the authority of the Church has been ordained for all living people.

It was prefigured in the Old Testament where human government is included in churchly authority; and it should be kept faithfully and firmly.

For the Old Testament extended till the time of the New, and from it sprang the greater precepts of the New Testament.

Thus from the lesser the greater was born.

For the Old Testament was the foundation, laid down in profoundest wisdom, that all might be built on it; and wisdom be made manifest in the Incarnation of the Son of God.

So the old wisdom lasted from the law of circumcision to the new rule of baptism, which was adorned with greater commands.

How secular and spiritual people are divided into four categories

The ways of living on earth are divided into those concerned with spiritual things and those concerned with secular life; and each way is divided into four categories.

God gave man the great power of reason that, inspired by the Holy Spirit, he might know these parts in himself after the pattern of the four elements.

The four parts pertain to both secular and spiritual life.

In secular affairs there are:

lesser and greater nobles, servants and followers.

In spiritual matters there are:

the excellent and the superior, the obeyers and the enforcers.

No one may seize, steal or buy spiritual or secular offices, for I establish them and want them to be used wisely and well. And by the ordinance of Providence these human distinctions exist forever.

Three kinds of people

There are three divisions between secular people:

Rulers.
Those free from the bonds of servitude.
Common people, subject to their governors.

Those who have spiritual authority and those appointed to govern should work in harmony and faith according to God's will, so that subjects are held in check.

But there must be a thoughtful justice in secular life, for the governors and those governed must touch one another in their joint labor and in a single-minded devotion of childlike innocence.

(Book 3: Vision 6)

THE PILLAR OF
THE TRINITY

"J saw in the west corner of the building a wondrous,
secret and supremely strong pillar, purple black in color.
It was so placed that it protruded both inside and outside the building ..."

(Hildegard's vision)

The pillar

T he pillar symbolizes the true Trinity. It is the perfect pillar of all good, reaching from the heights to the depths and governing the whole of this earthly globe.

It stands in the west corner of the building because the Son of God was incarnate in the sunset of the world.

He glorified the Father everywhere, and promised the Holy Spirit to His disciples.

So too the Son, undergoing death by the will of the Father, gave humans a noble example, so that they too could rightfully enter the building of the Supreme Father by performing good works in the Holy Spirit.

And the pillar is wonderfully secret and supremely strong. For God is made manifest so wonderfully in His creatures that they can never exhaust all that can be known about Him; neither can they understand Him by human strength when contrasted with the divine strength.

The pillar's color of purple and black signifies the purple blood poured out by the Son on behalf of humans with their black sins.

Thus the Son saved the world by His Passion and brought the true and right faith to believers.

When the old rituals failed a new holiness arose in the worship of the Trinity. For it was made clear that the Father sent His Son, conceived by the Holy Spirit into the world.

And the Son sought, not His own glory, but the glory of the Father.

He also showed the consolations of the Holy Spirit which had been foretold.

Thus the pillar protrudes both inside and outside the building, for truth was proclaimed alike to right living believers and non-believers outside the faith.

(Book 3: Vision 7)

THE SYMPHONY OF THE BLESSED

"Then I saw the clear sky, in which I heard different kinds of music, marvelously embodying all the meaning I had heard before. I heard the praises of the joyful citizens of Heaven, steadfastly persevering in the ways of the truth. I heard laments, calling people back to these praises and joys …"

(Hildegard's vision)

The praises of the blessed

I heard the multitude making music in harmony and praising the ranks of heaven in these words:

Songs to holy Mary

O sweet green branch that flowers from the stem of
Jesse!
O glorious thing, that God on his fairest daughter
Looked as the eagle looks at the face of the sun!
The Most High Father sought for the Virgin's candor,
And willed that His Word should take from her His
body.
For the Virgin's mind was by His mystery illumined,
And from her virginity sprang the glorious Flower.

To the nine orders of the heavenly spirits

O glorious living light, which lives in Divinity!
Angels who fix your eyes with ardent desire
Amid the mystical darkness surrounding all crea-
tures
On Him, with whom your desires can never be sated!

Praise be to you all, who behold the heart of the Father,
And see the Ancient of Days spring forth in the fountain.
And His inner power appears like a face from Heaven.

To the patriarchs and prophets

O eminent men, who traversed the hidden ways,
And looked with the eyes of the spirit, and in lucent shadows
Announced the Living Light that would bud from the stem
Which blossomed alone from the Light that was rooted within it.

(Hymns follow to the apostles, the martyrs, the confessors and the virgins).

A lament for those who had to be recalled to that place

O Living Fountain, how great was Your sweet compassion!
You never lost sight of the face of the straying people.
But saw in advance the way that You would save them
From the fallen angels, who thought they had taken them from You.
O daughter of Zion, rejoice that God restores to you
So many cut off by the ancient serpent,
yet who now shine brighter than ever they shone before.

How God must be praised without ceasing

Praises must be offered to the Supernal Creator with heart and mouth, for by His grace He sets on heavenly thrones not only those who stand erect, but also those who bend and fall.

For the song of rejoicing, sung in unity and in concord, tells of the glory and honor of the citizens of Heaven, and lifts on high what the Word has shown.

And so the words symbolize the body.
The jubilant music indicates the spirit.
The celestial harmony shows the Divinity, while the words show the Humanity of the Son of God.

Therefore, let everyone who understands God by faithful faith, offer Him tireless praises, and with joyful devotion sing to Him without ceasing.

Praise therefore, praise God, you blessed hearts, for the miracles which God has wrought in the frail earthly reflection of the beauty of the Most High (the human race).
This He foreshadowed when He first made Woman from the rib of the man He had created.

But let the one who has sharp ears to hear inner meanings, ardently love My reflection and pant after My words, inscribing them in the soul and in the conscience. Amen.

FOR FURTHER READING

Texts and Anthologies

Hildegard of Bingen — Scivias: Translated by Mother Columba Hart and Jane Bishop. Classics of Western Spirituality. Mahwah, NJ: Paulist Press, 1990.

Hildegard of Bingen — Secrets of God: Writings of Hildegard of Bingen. Selected and translated by Sabina Flanagan. Boston & London: Shambala Press, 1996.

Hildegard of Bingen — An Anthology. Edited and Introduced by Fiona Bowie and Oliver Davies. London: SPCK, 1990.

Hildegard of Bingen — A Spiritual Reader. Carmen Acevedo Butcher; Brewster, MA: Paraclete Press, 2007.

Related Works

Barry, Patrick, OSB. *Saint Benedict's Rule*: translated and with an introduction. Mahwah, NJ: Paulist Press, 1985.

Furlong, Monica (Editor). *Feminine in the Church*. London: SPCK, 1984.

Graef, Hilda. *The Story of Mysticism*. London: Peter Davies, 1966.

Hamilton, Lisa B. *Wisdom from the Middle Ages for Middle Aged Women*. New York: Morehouse Publishing, 2007.

Lyddon, Eileen. *Mysticism for Beginners: John of the Cross Made Easy.* New York: New City Press, 2006.

McGinn, Bernard. *The Growth of Mysticism.* New York: Herder, 1999.

Obbard, Elizabeth Ruth (Editor). *Medieval Women Mystics.* New York: New City Press, 2007.

Ranft, Patricia. *Women and Spiritual Equality in the Christian Tradition.* New York: St. Martin's Press, 1998.